This Coloring Book Belongs to:

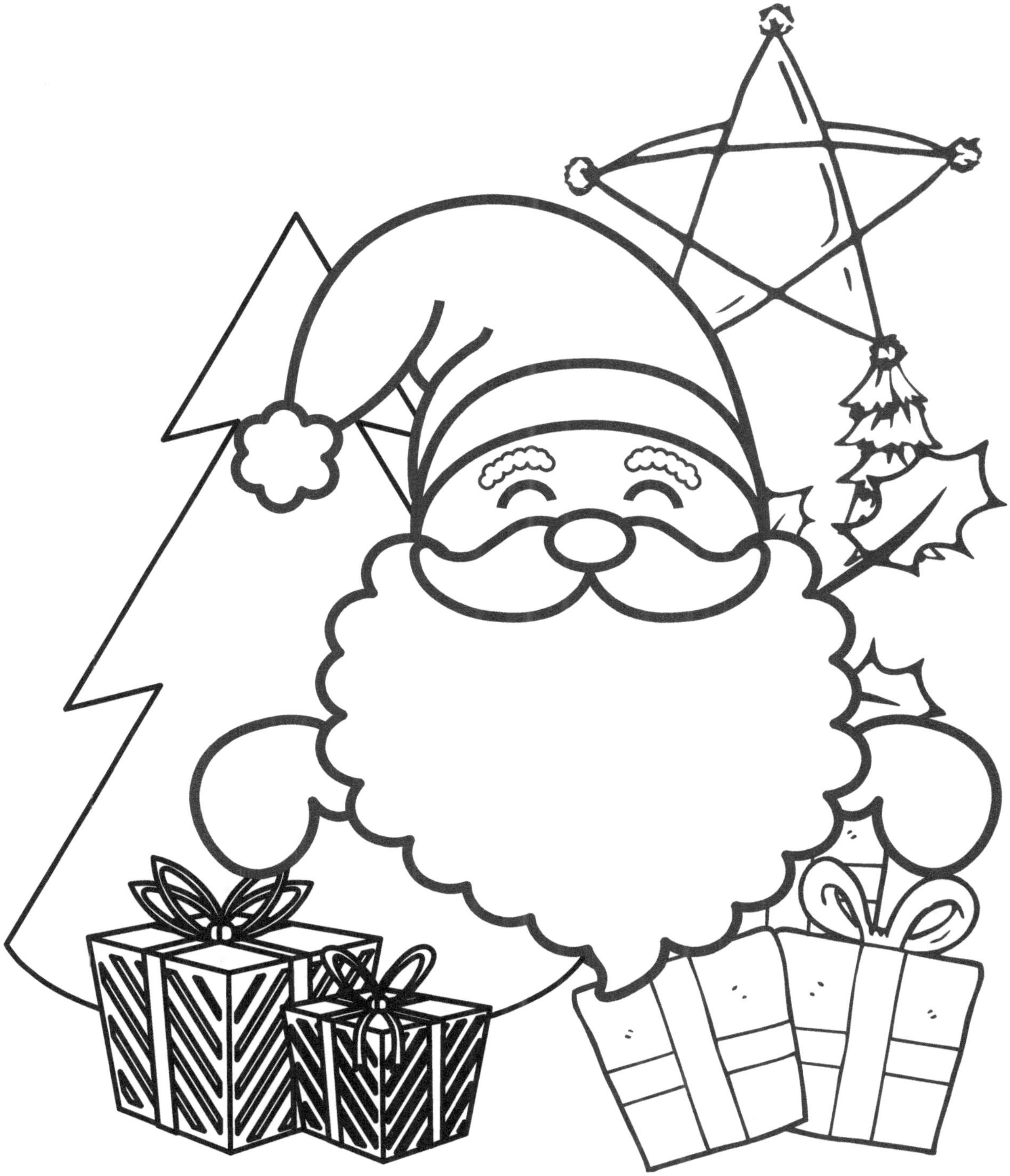

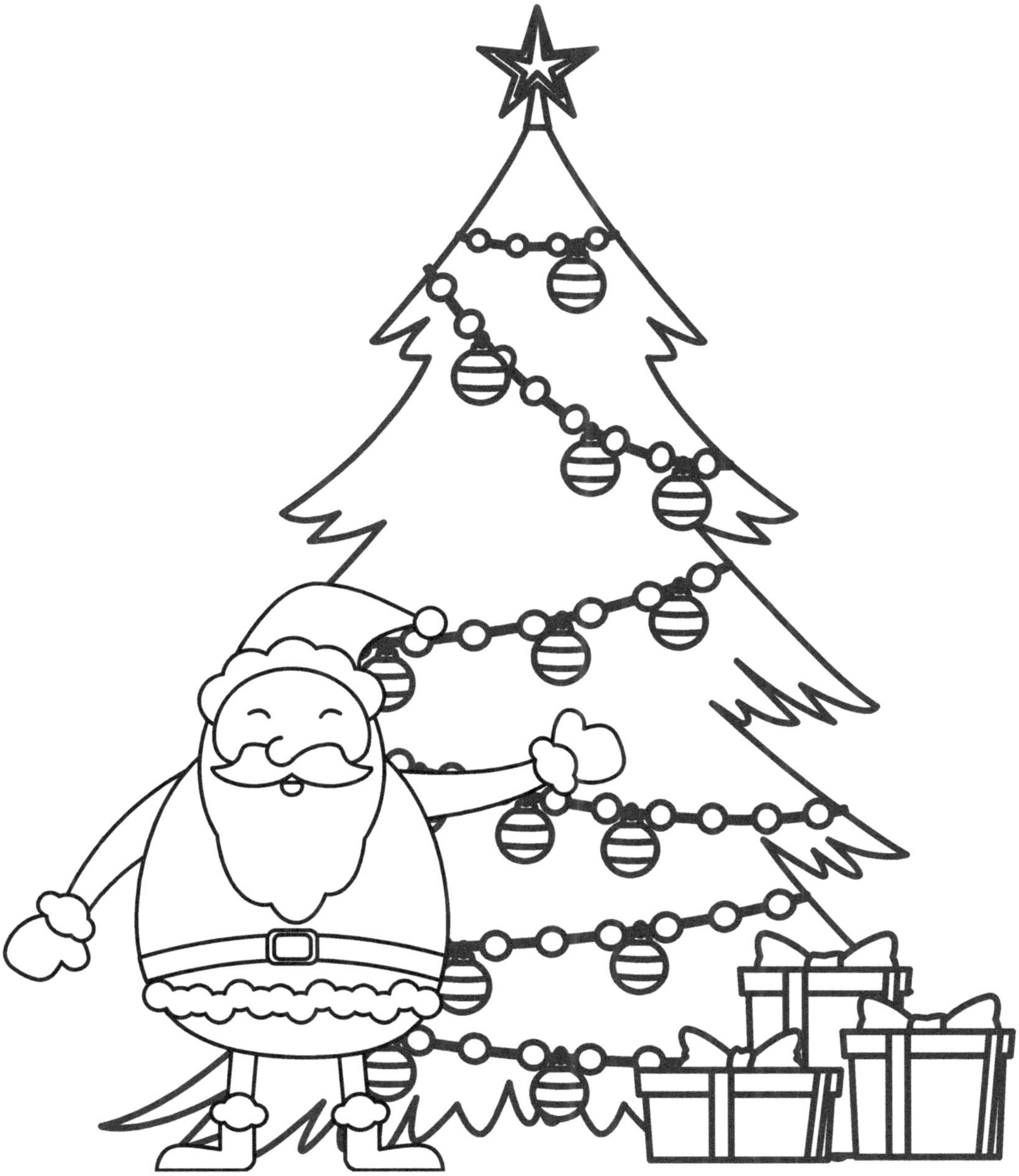

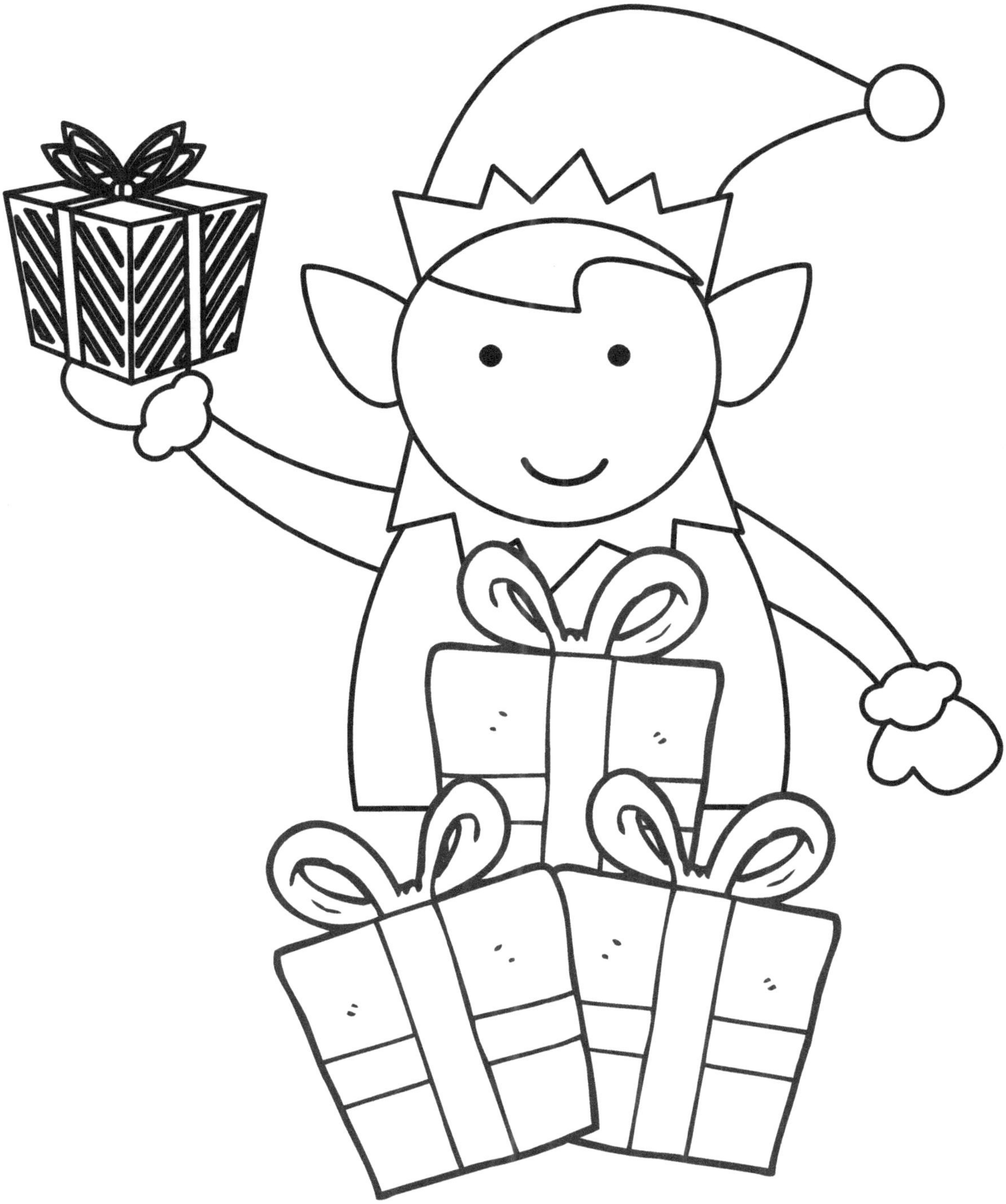

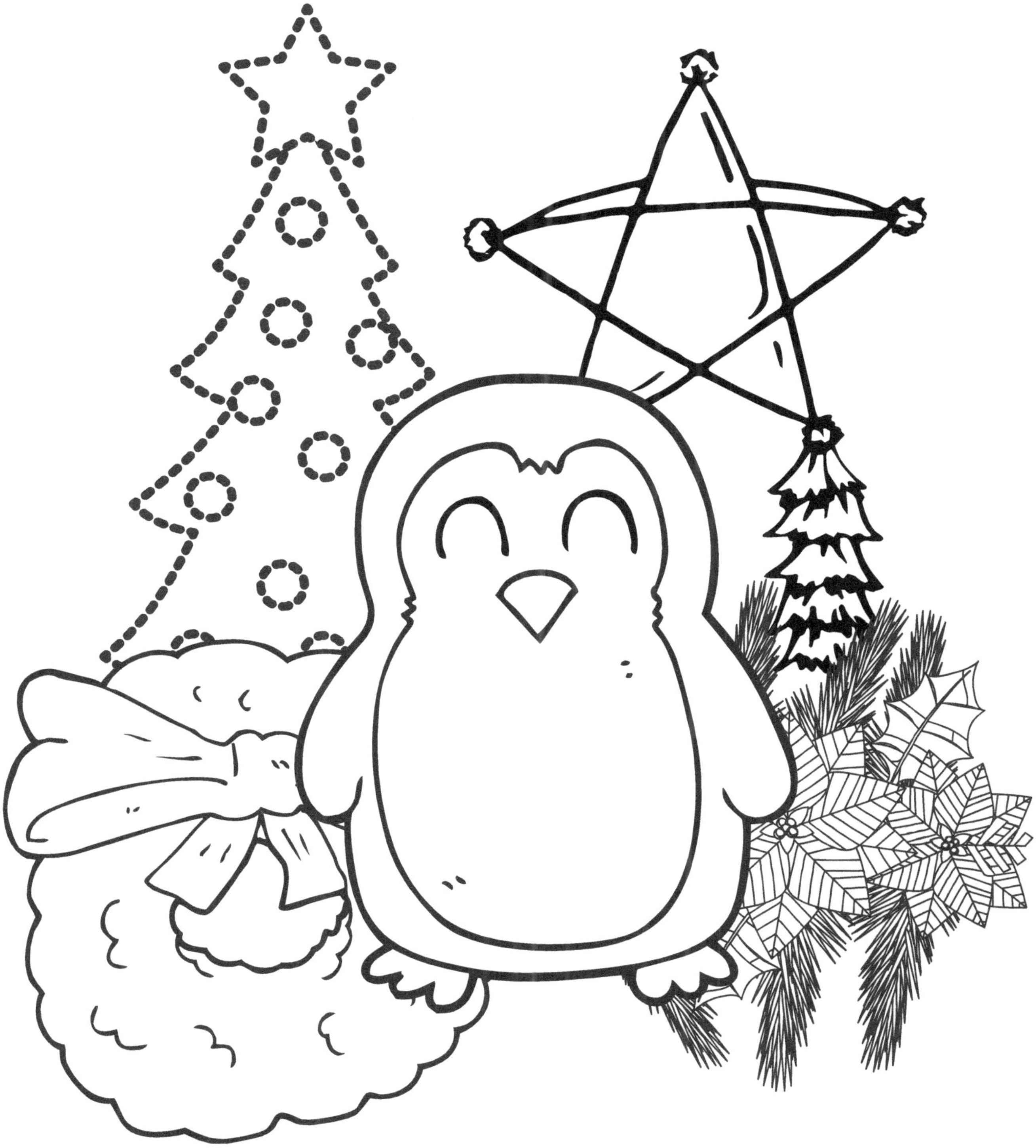

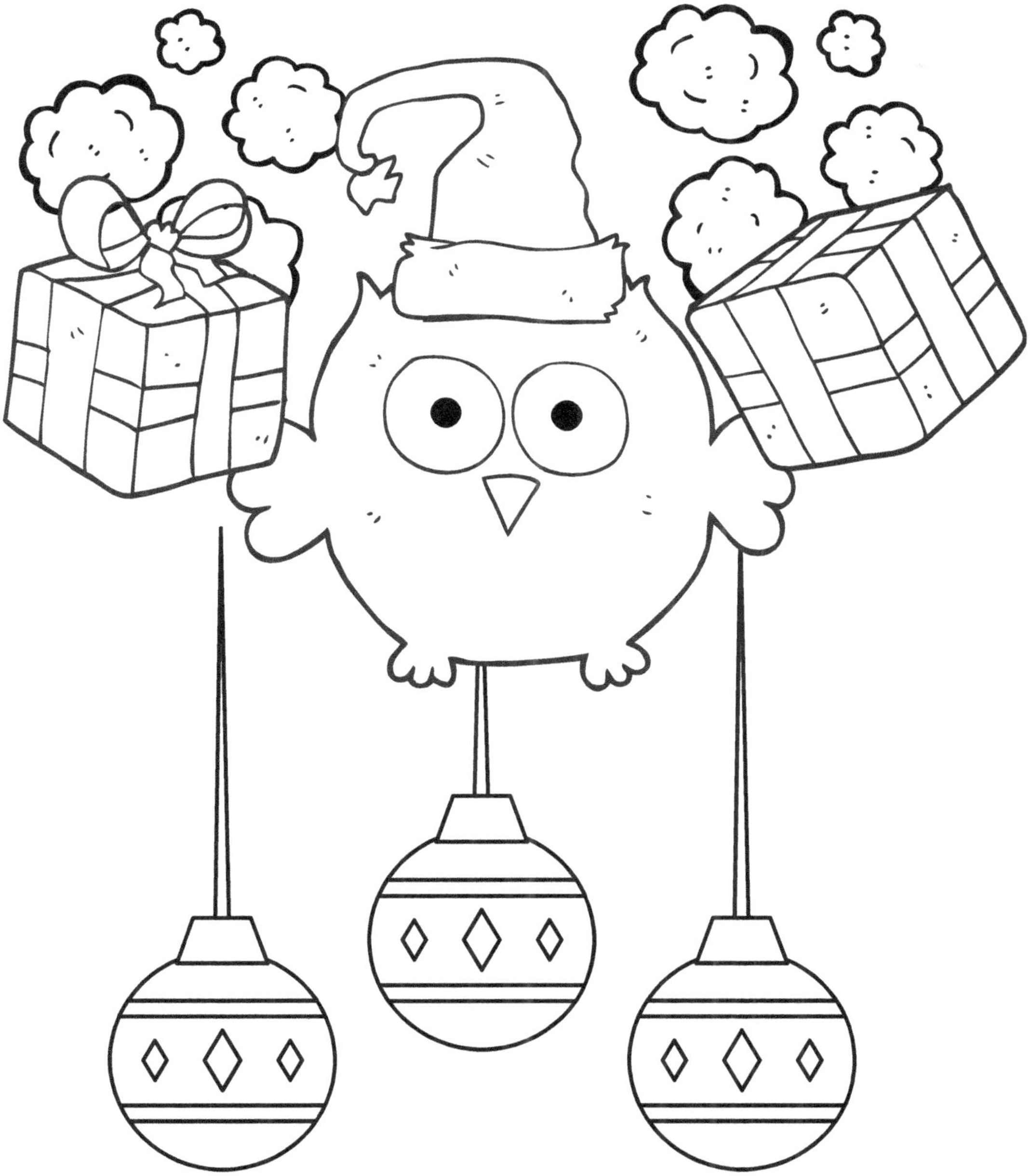

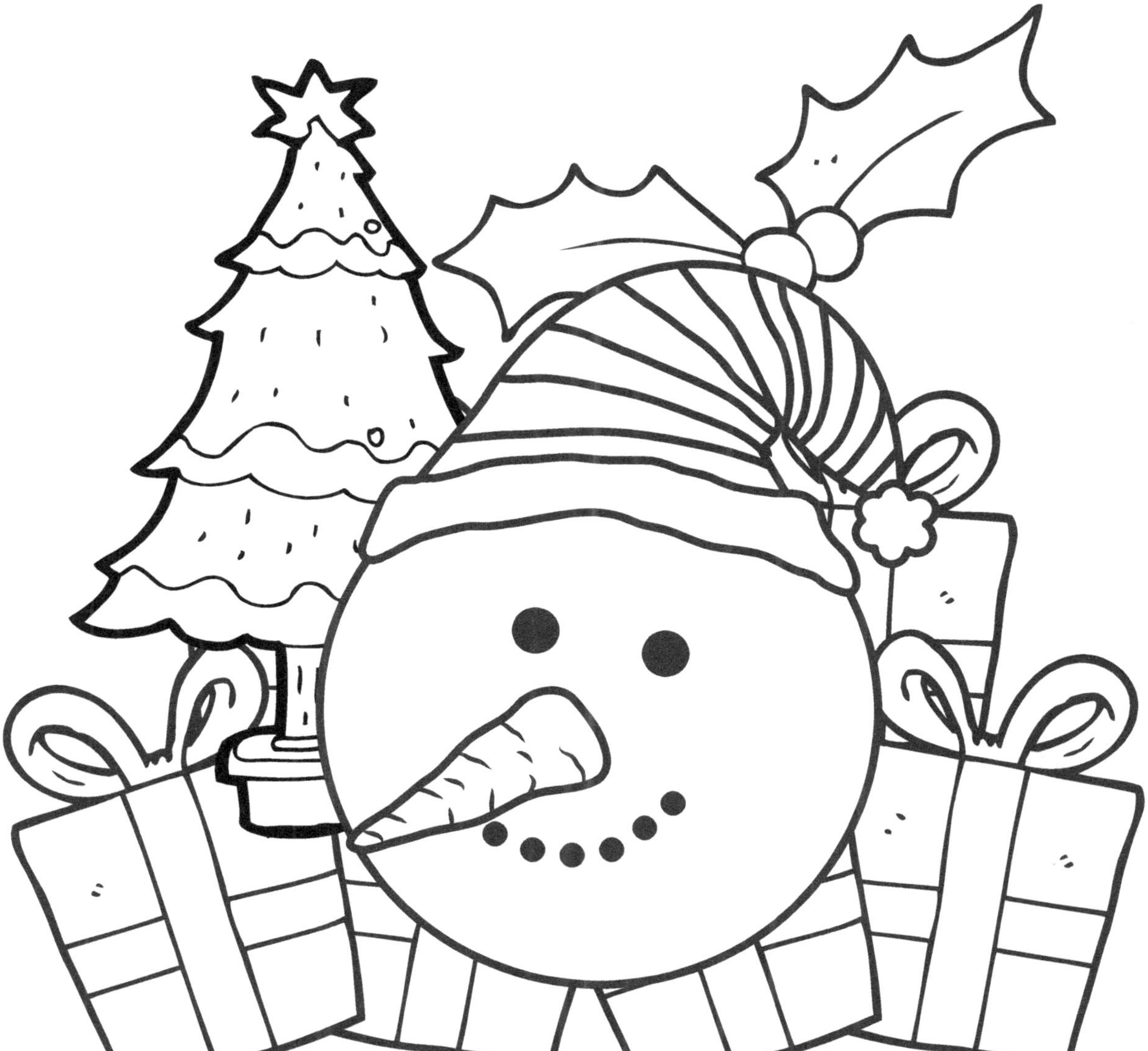

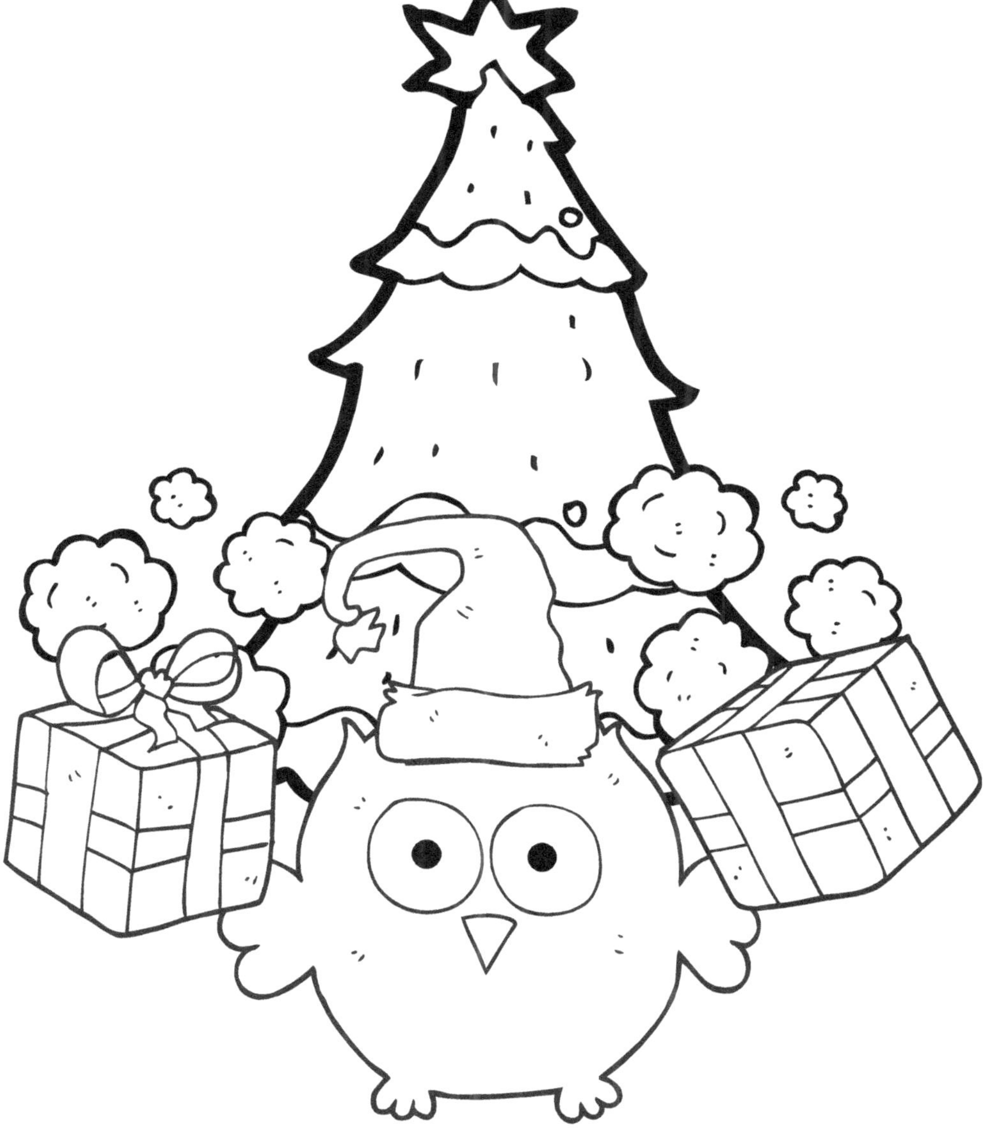

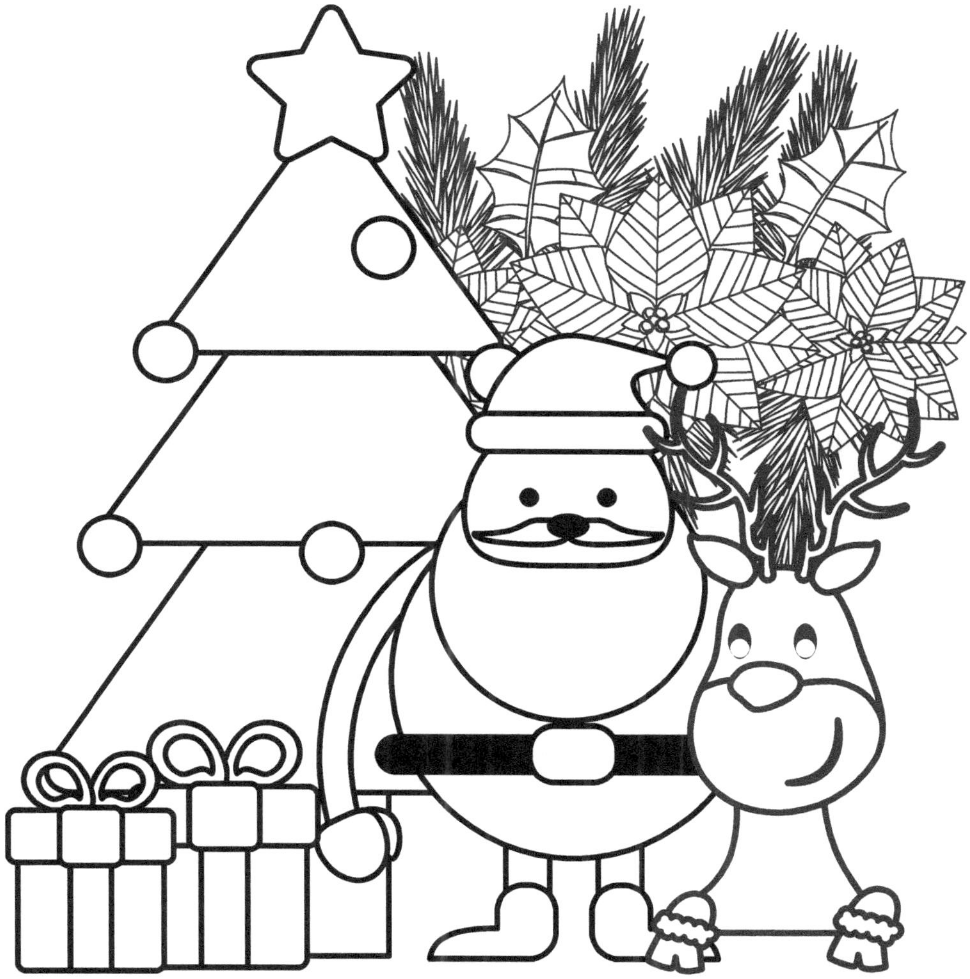

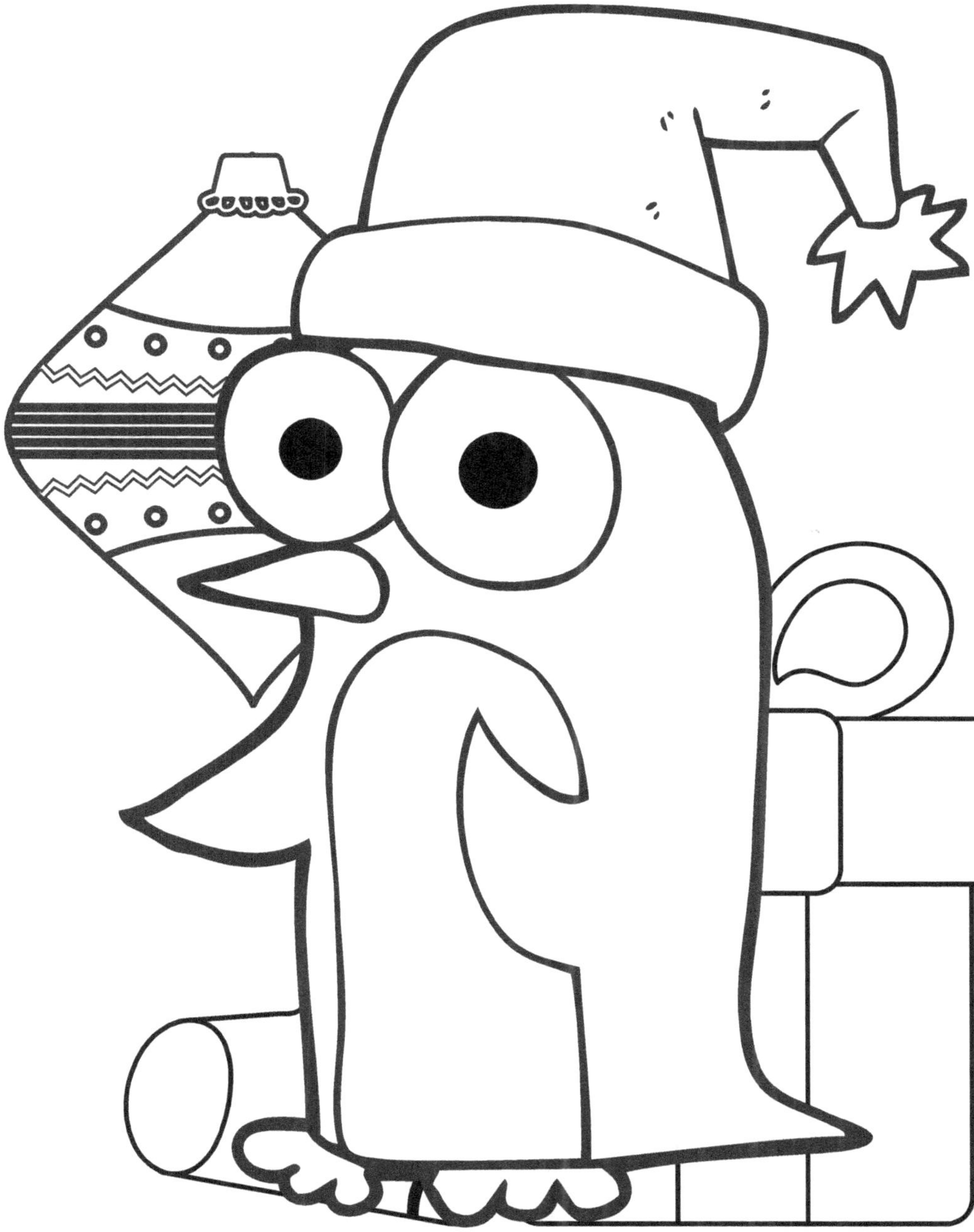

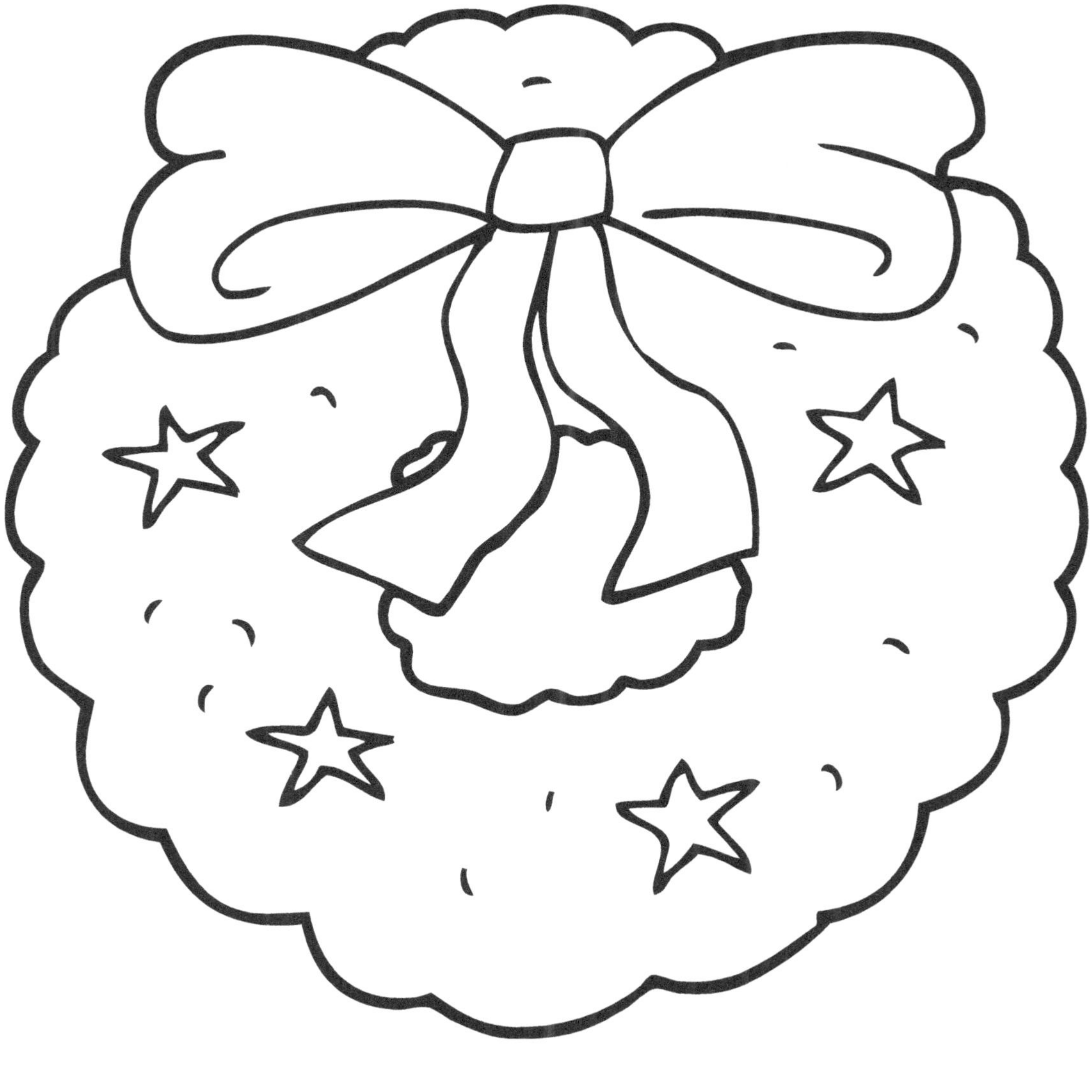

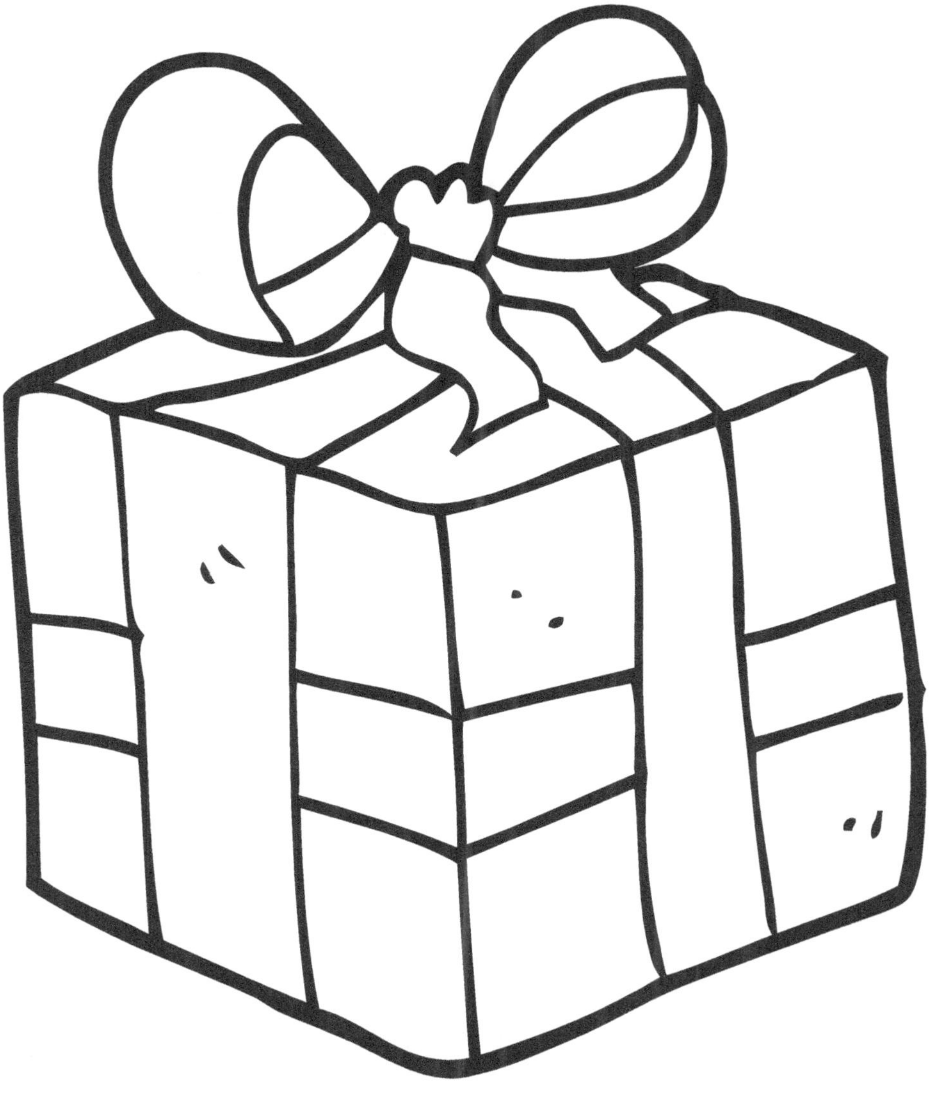

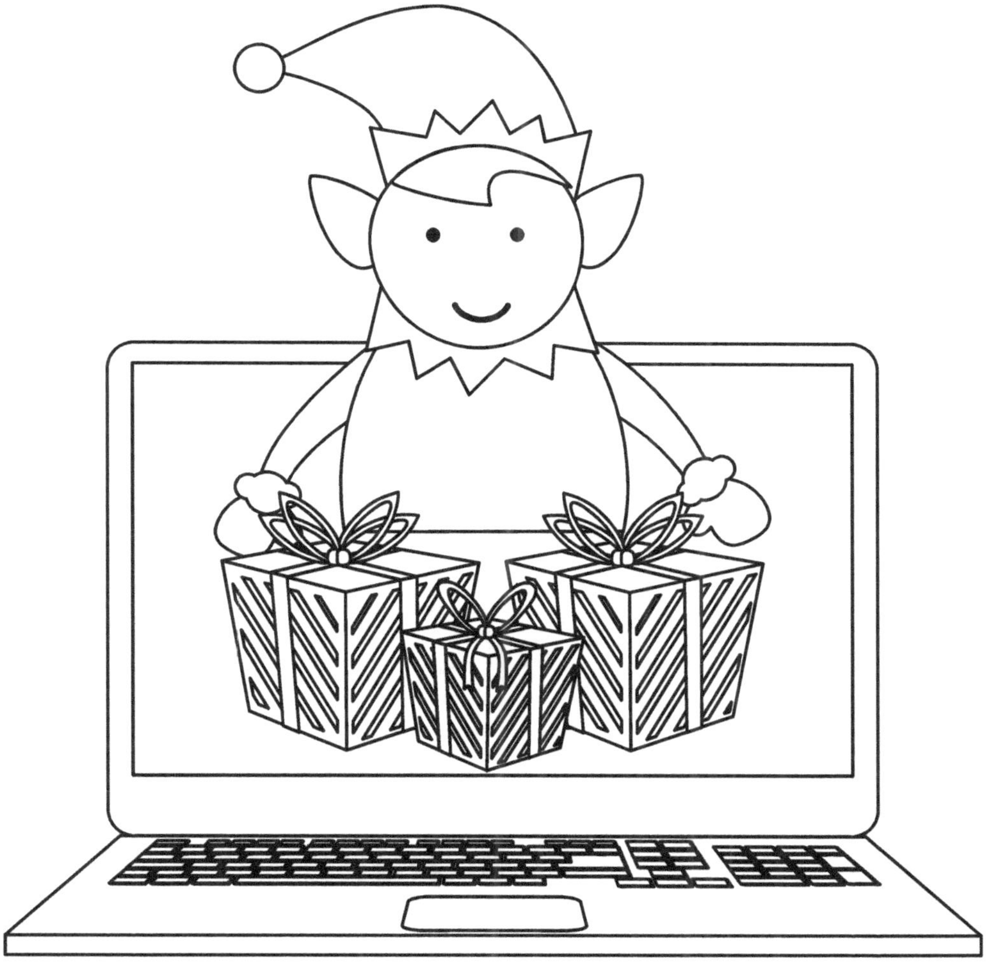

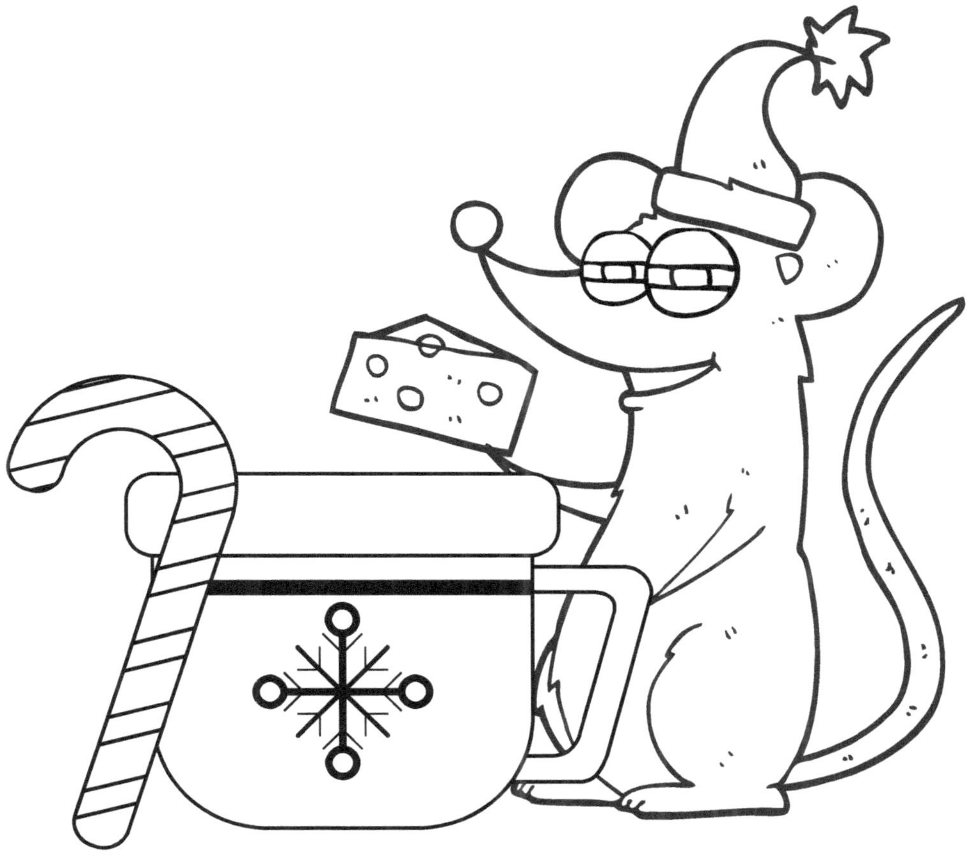

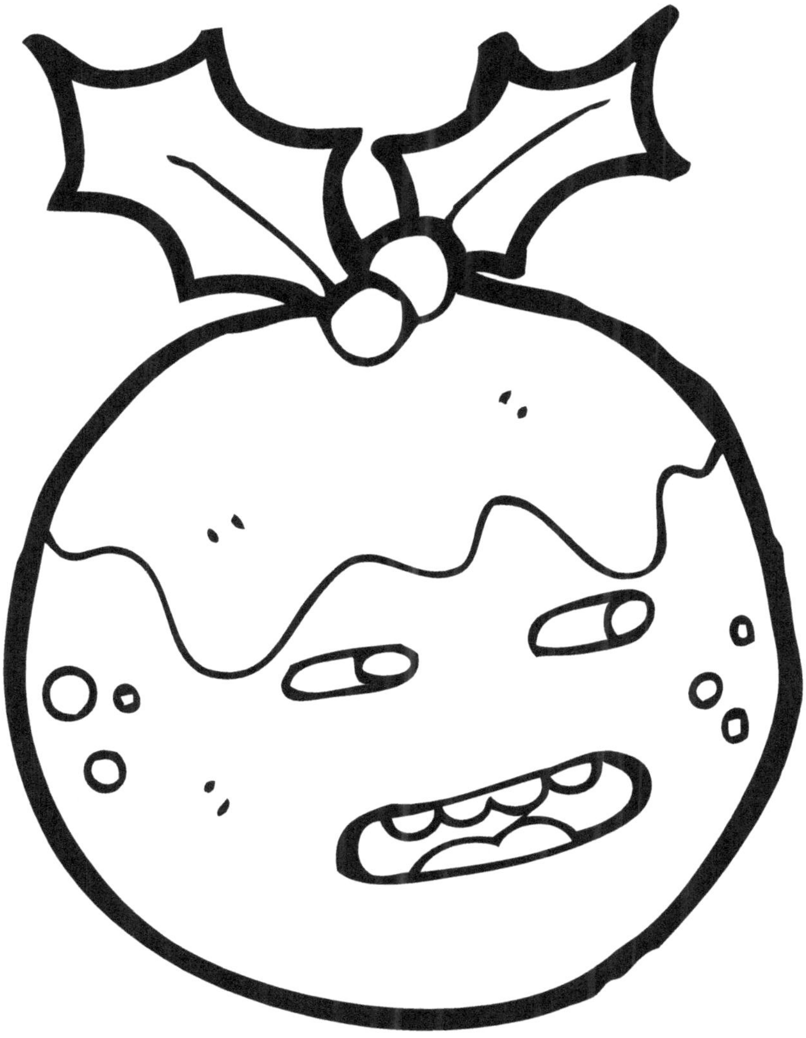

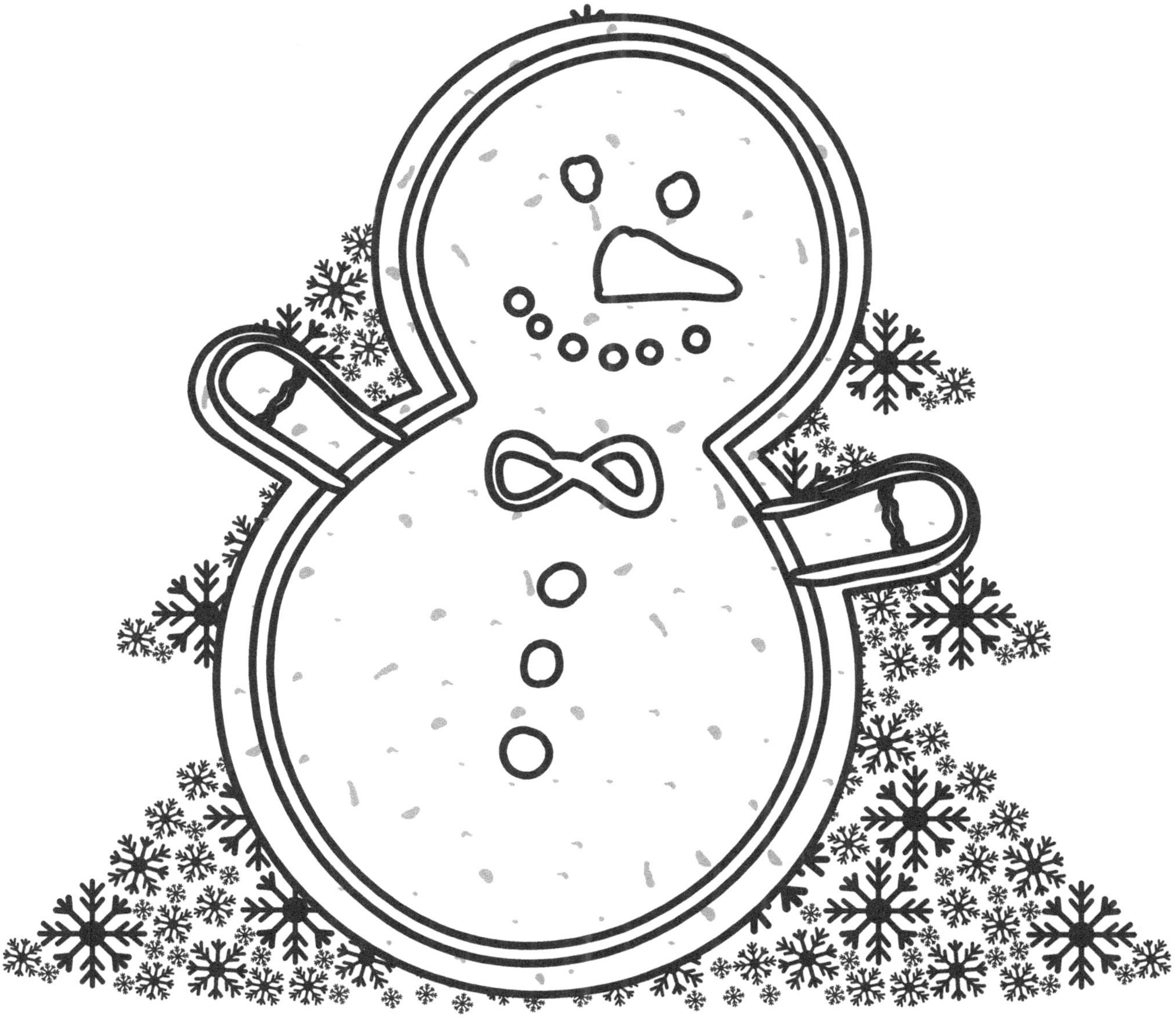

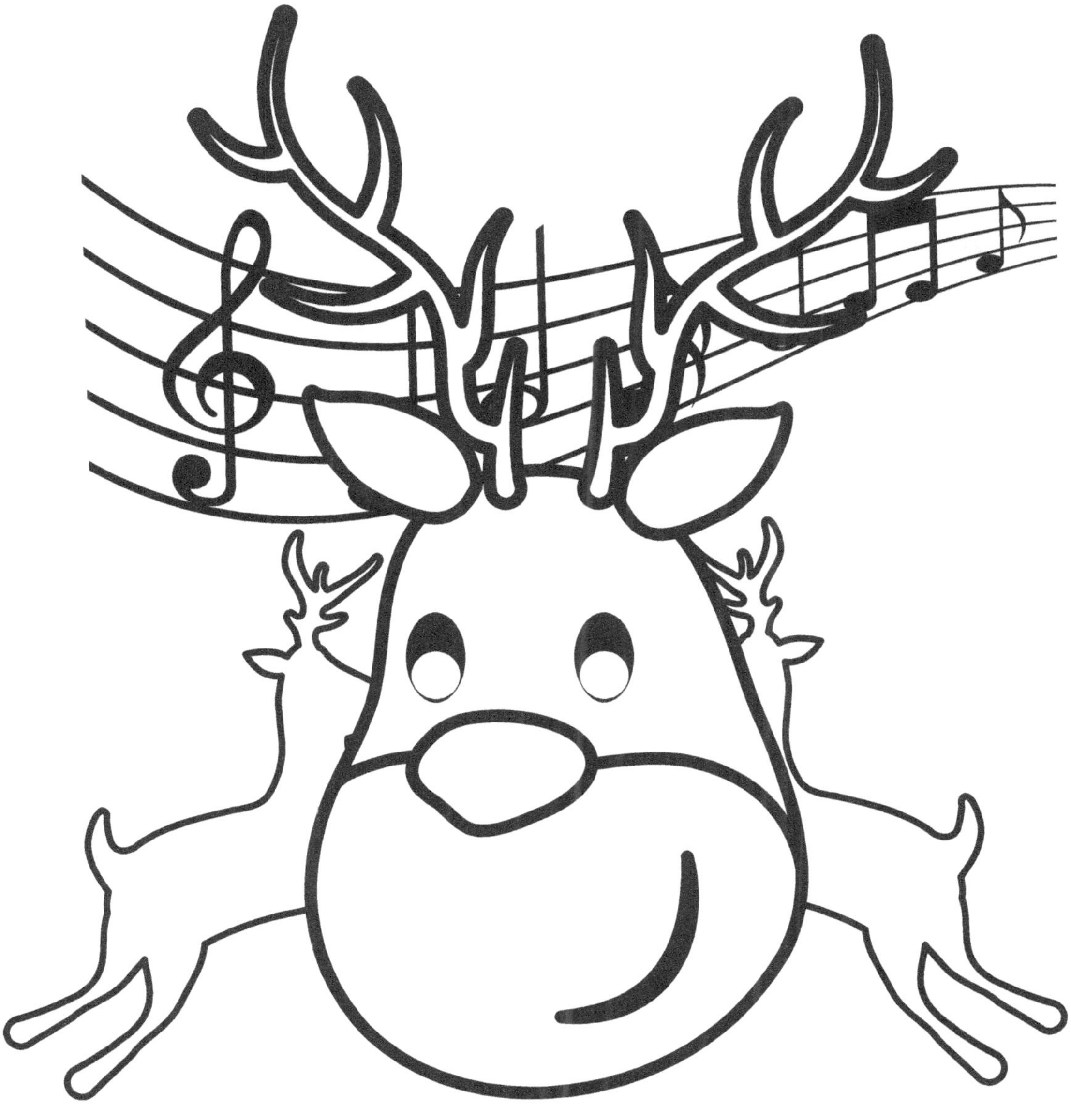

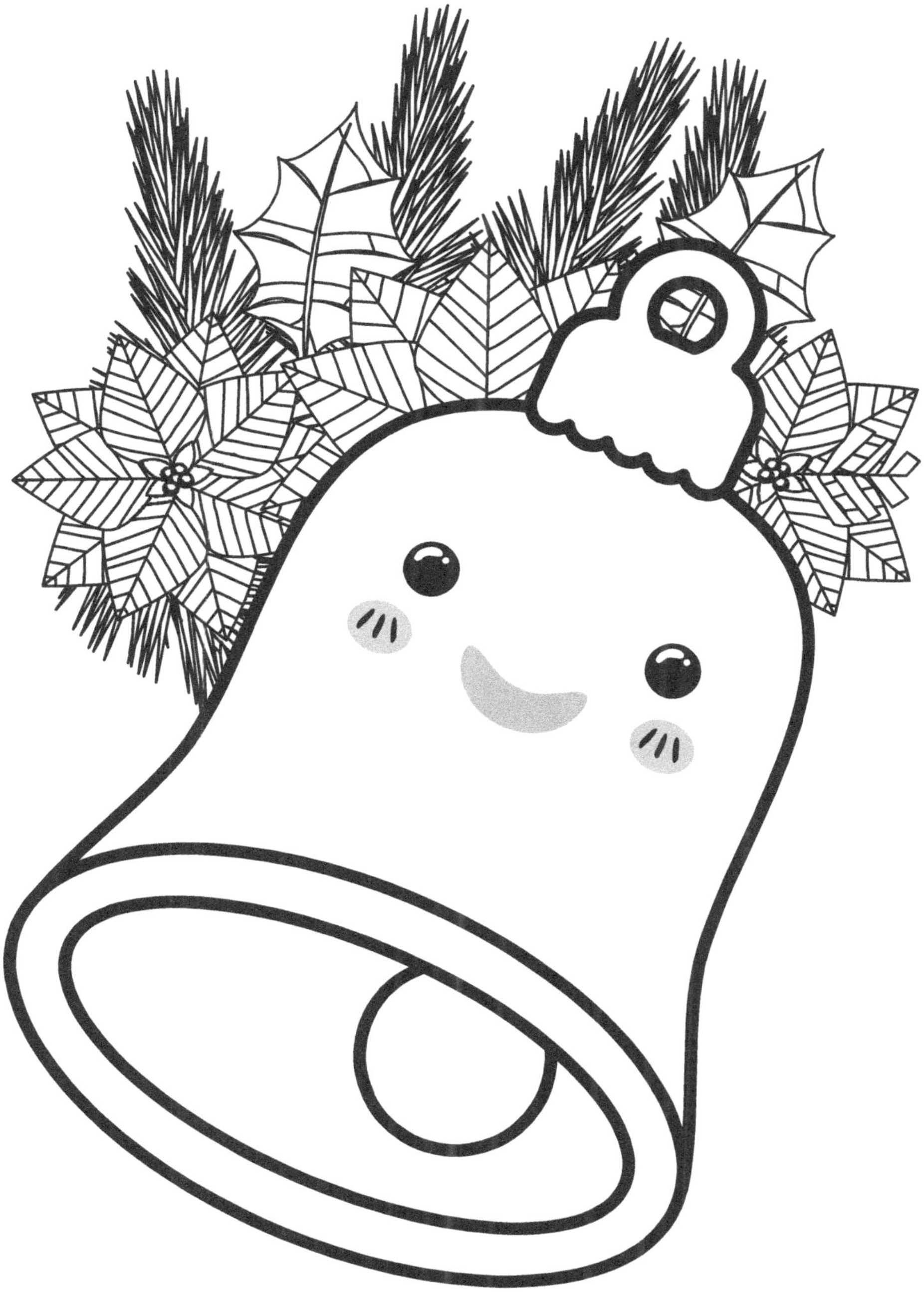

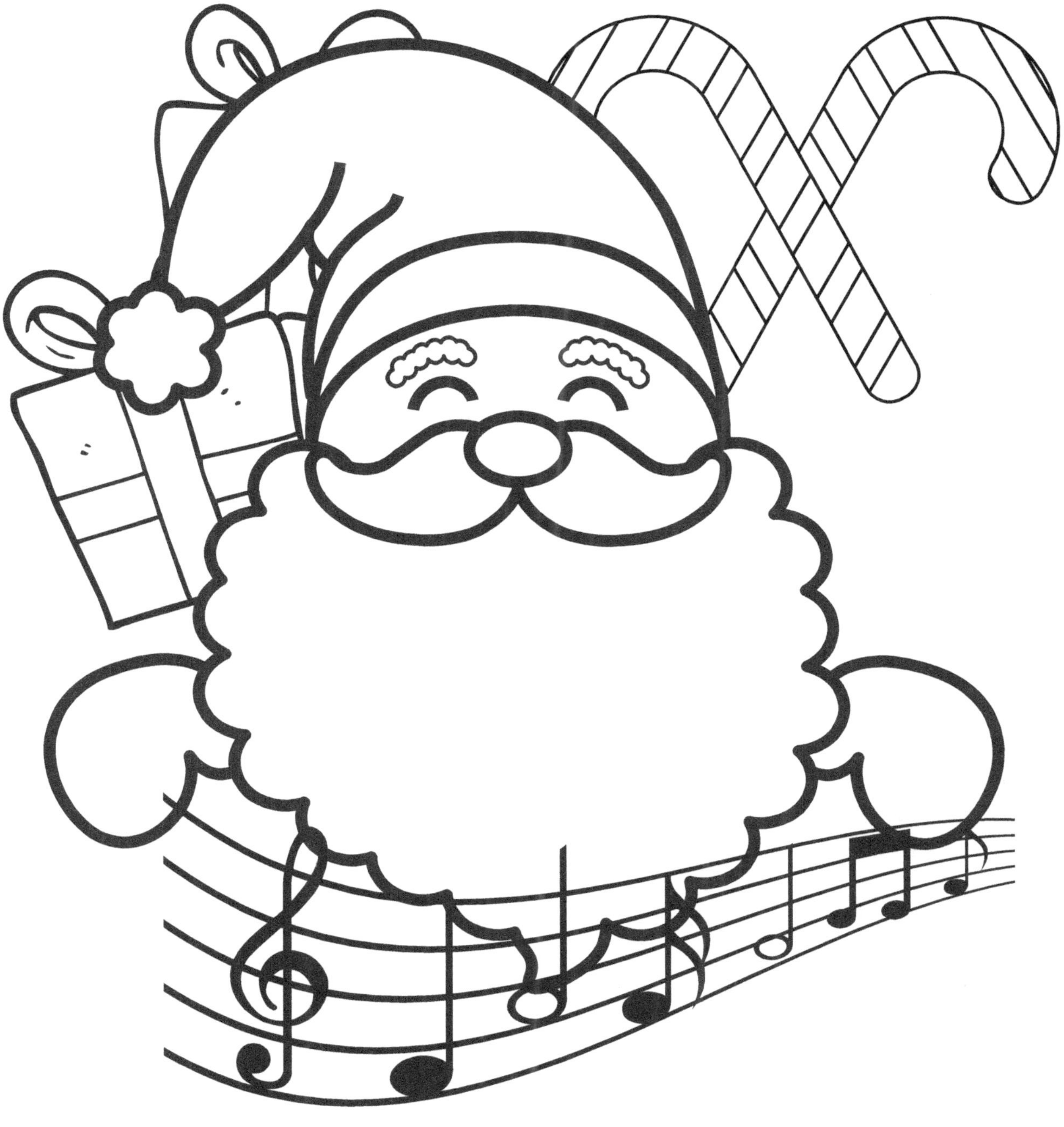

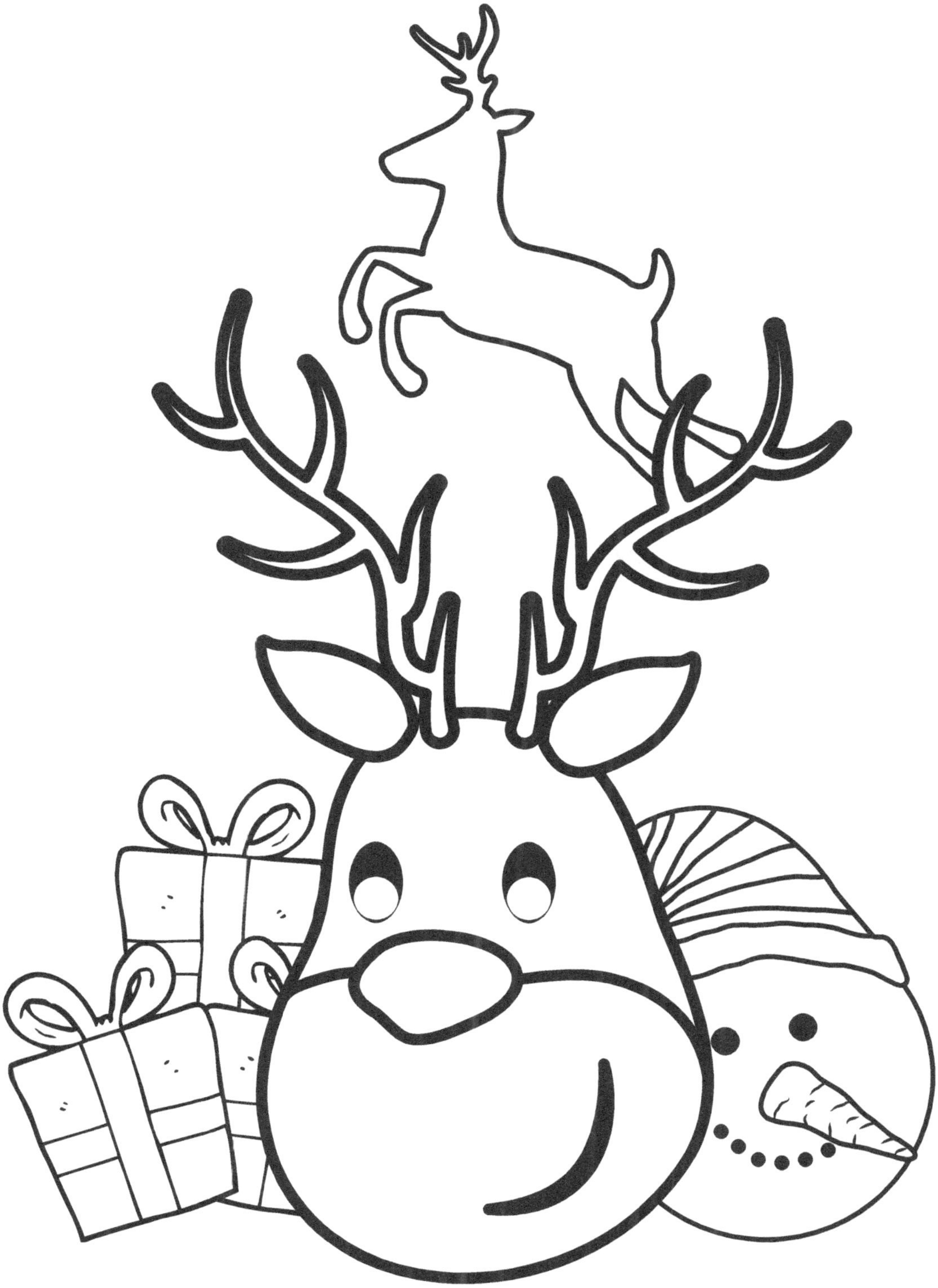

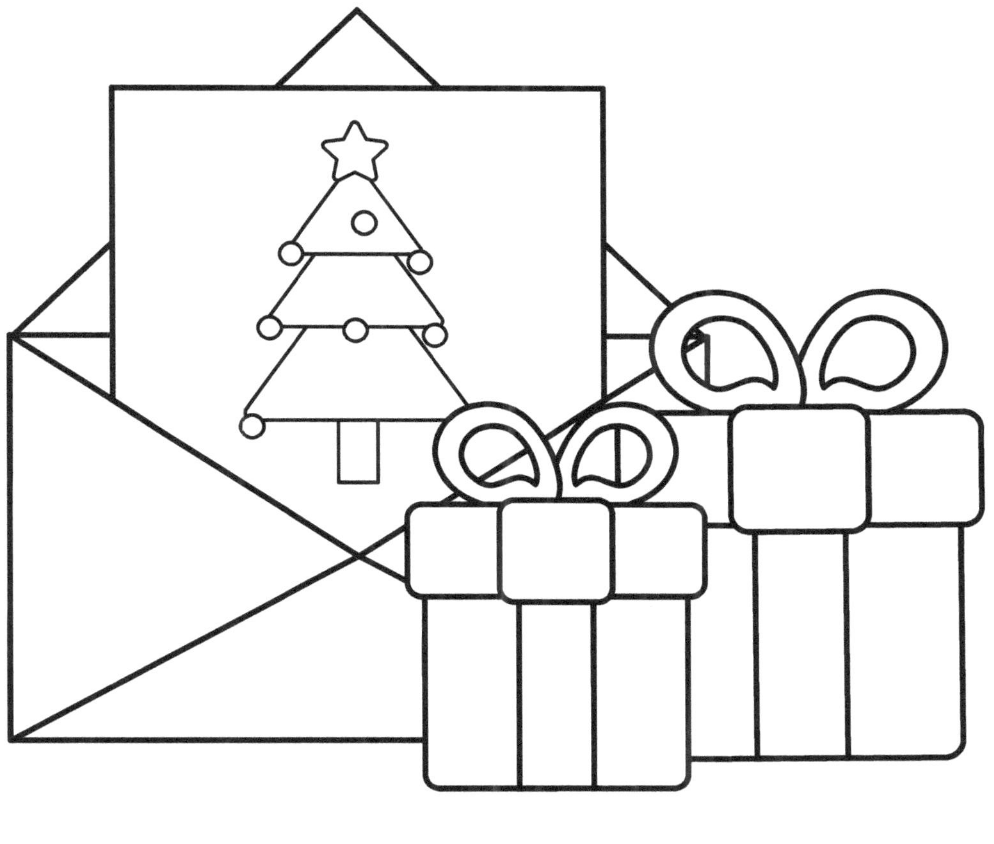

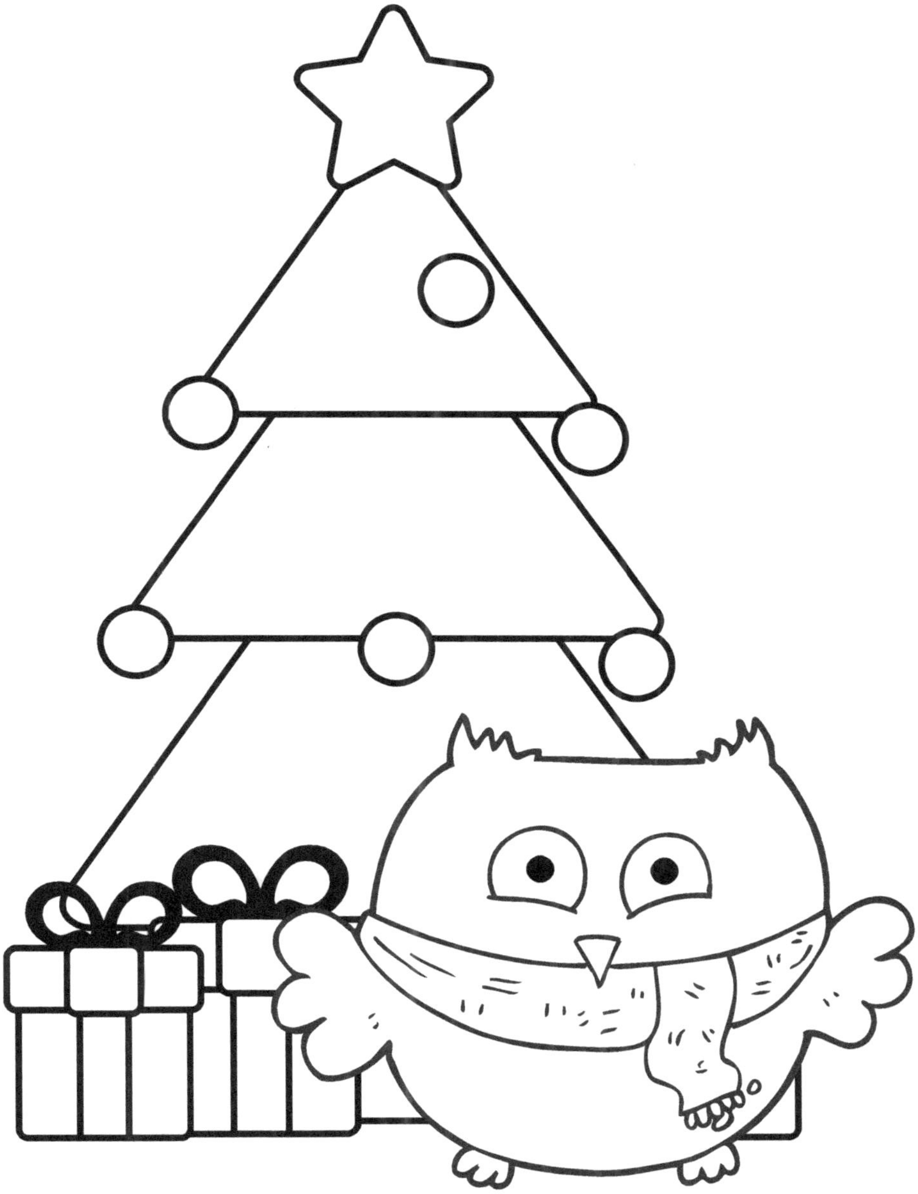

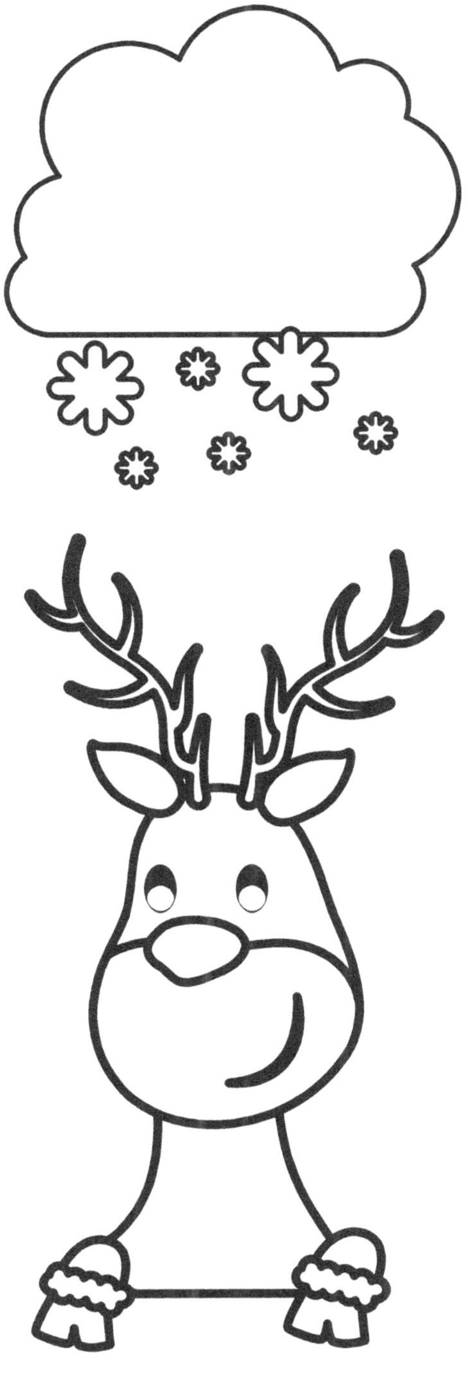

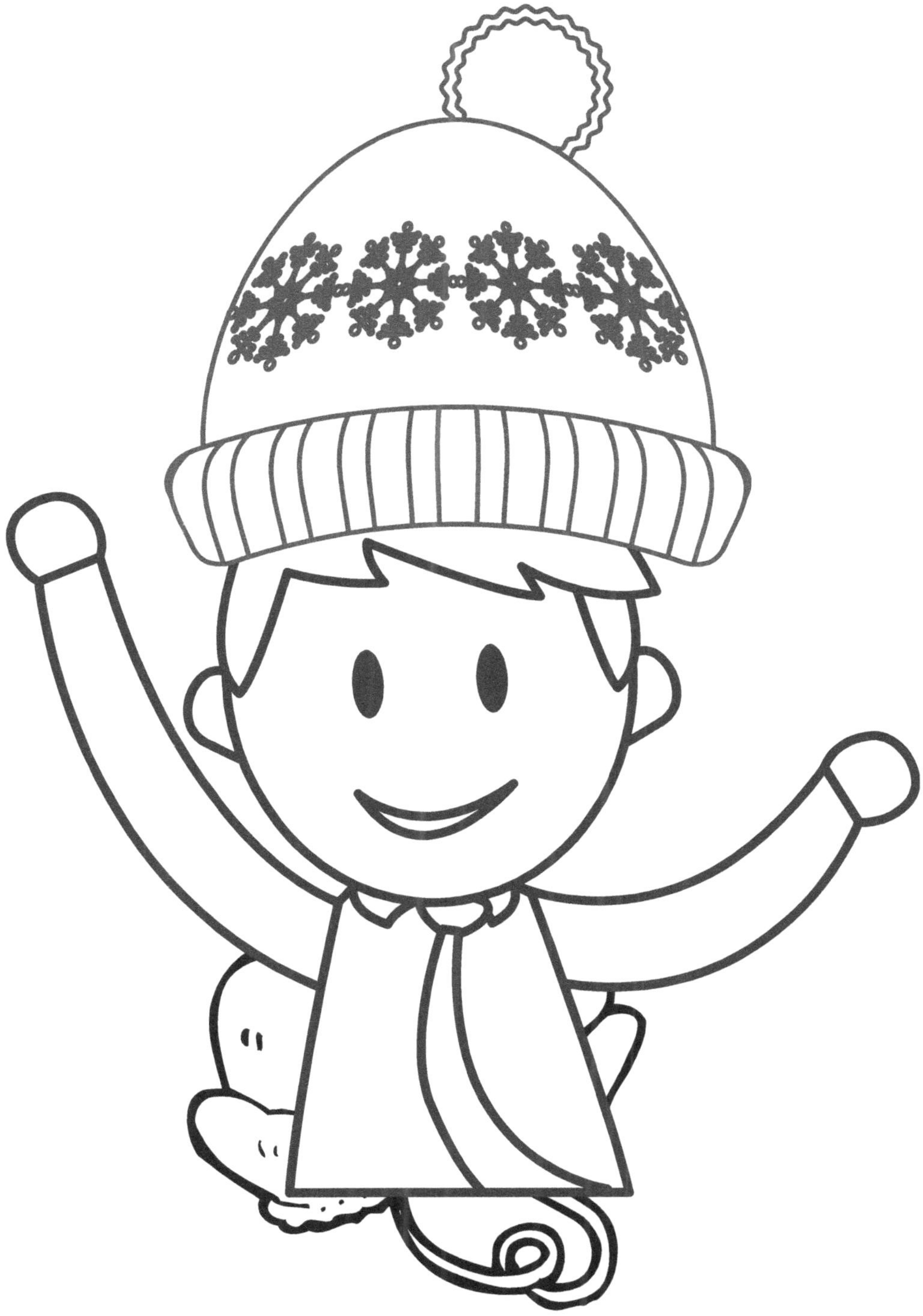

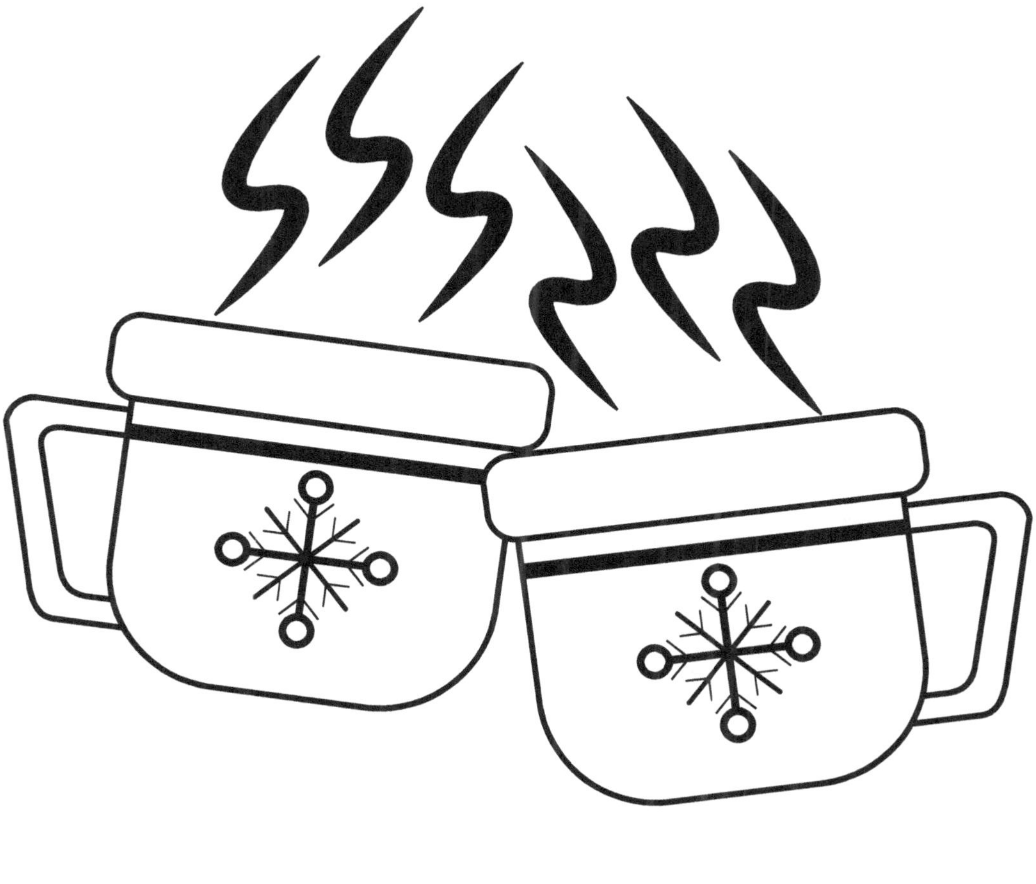

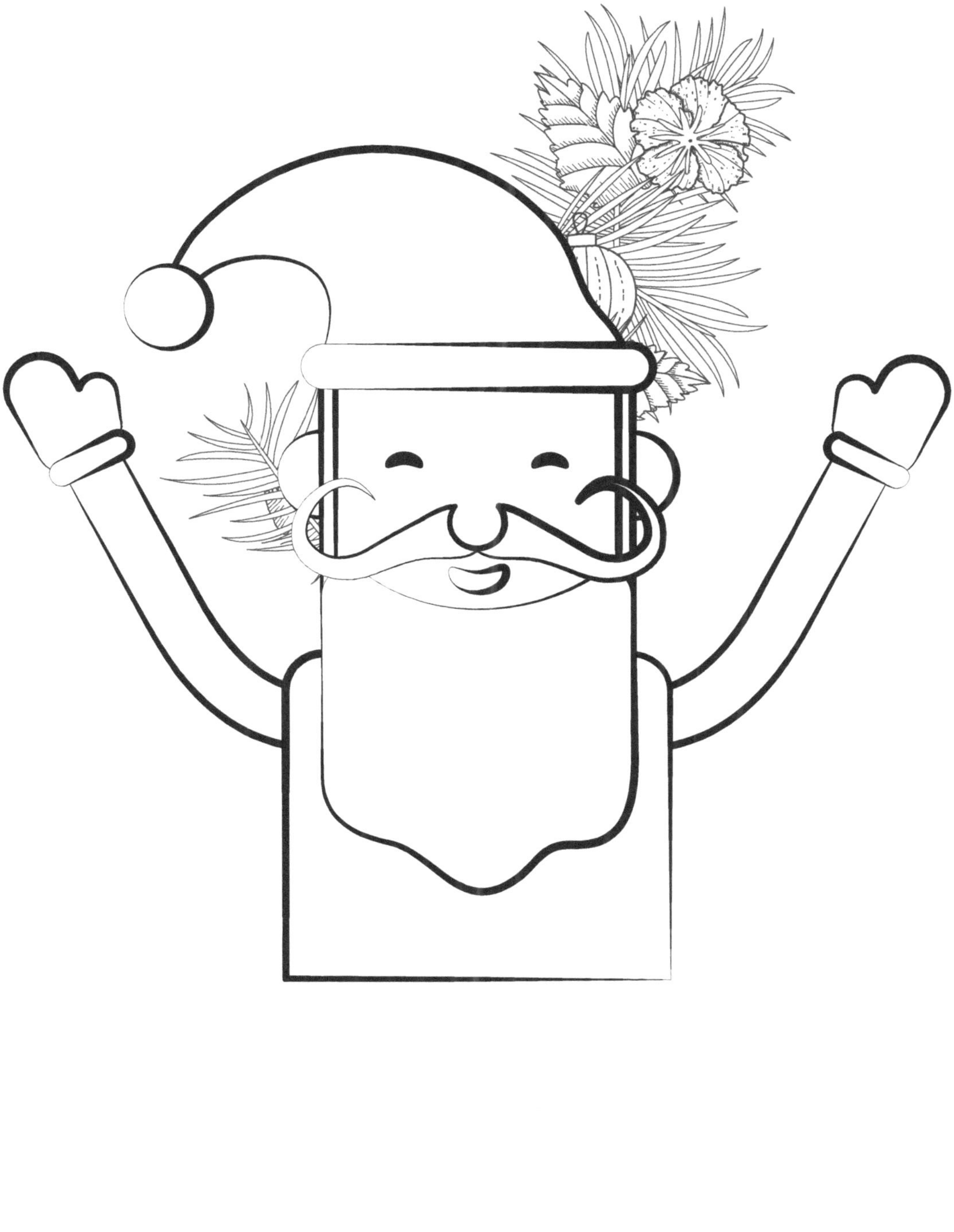

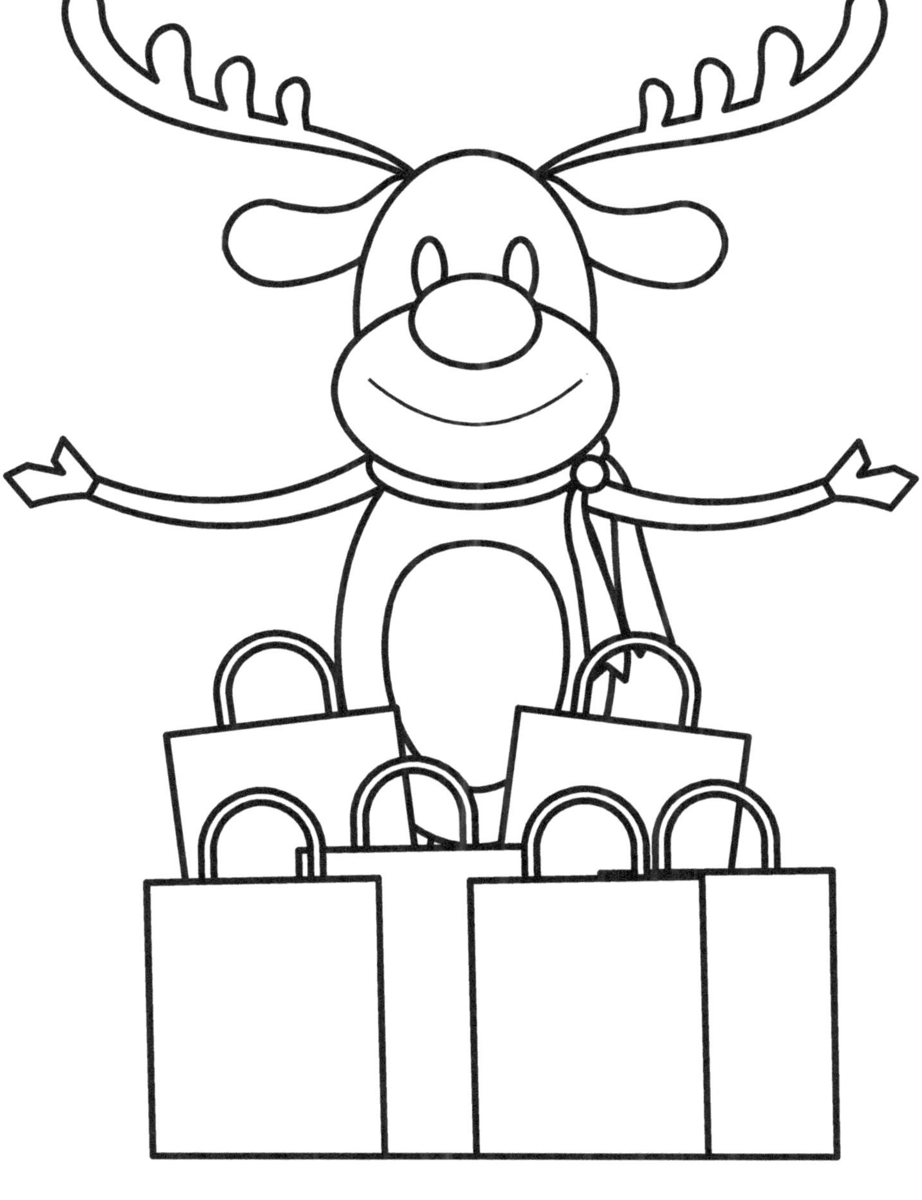

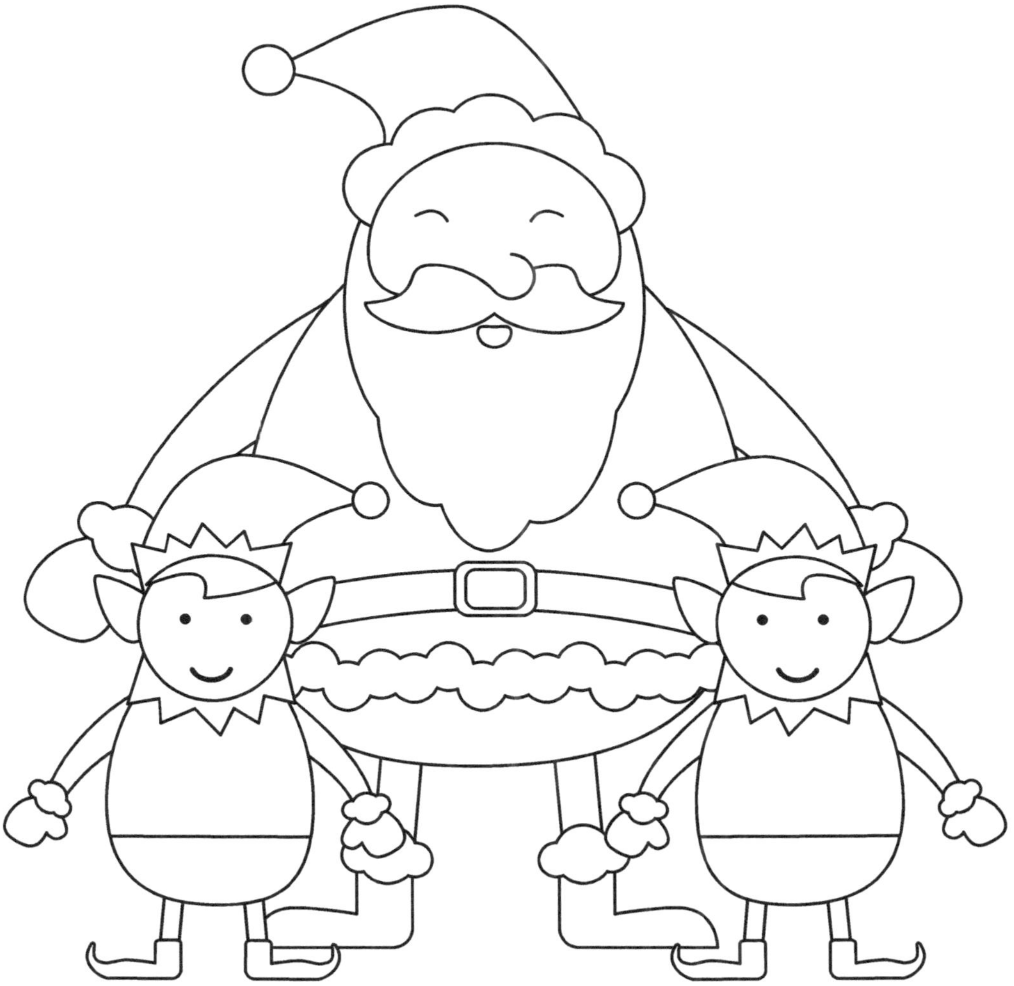

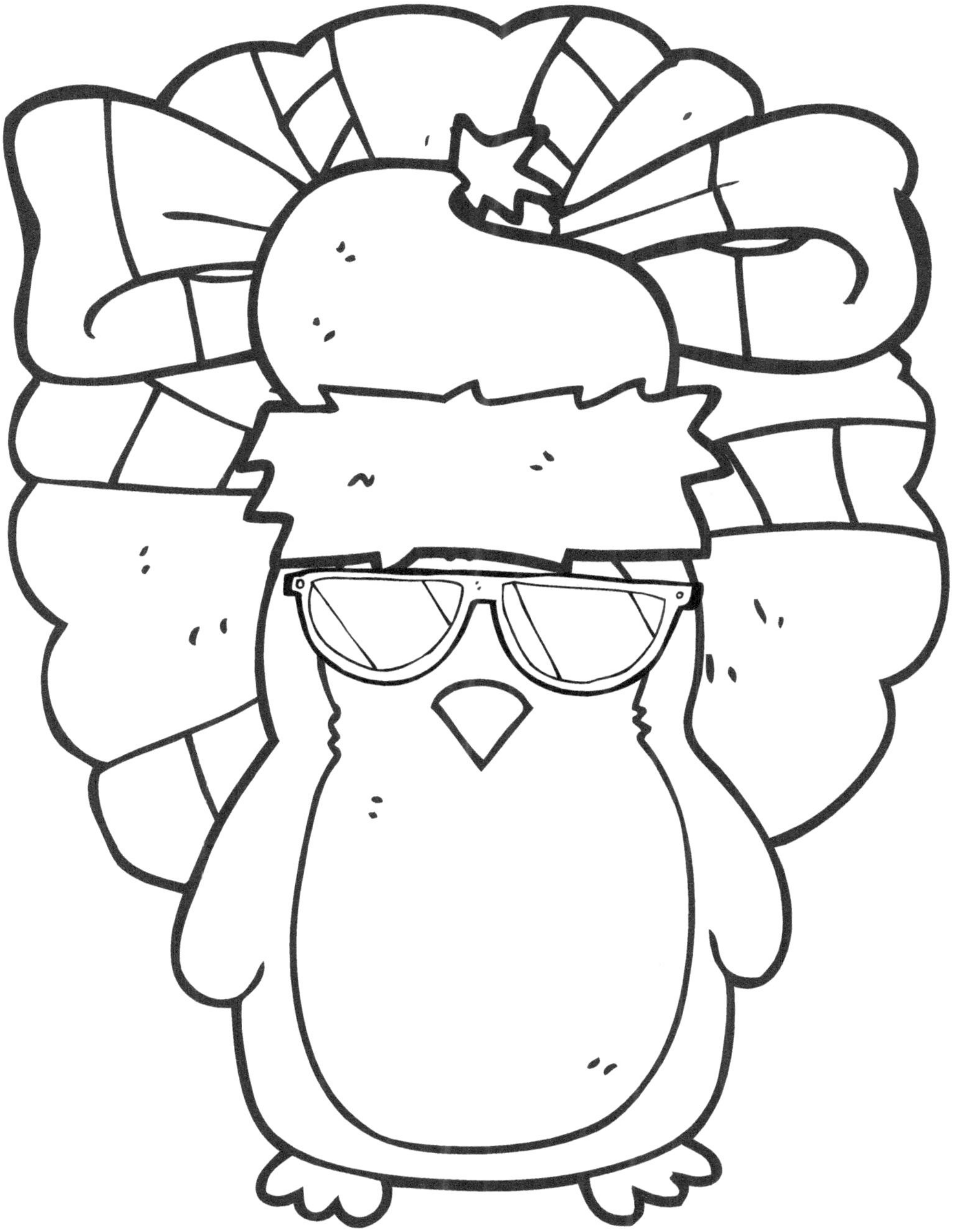

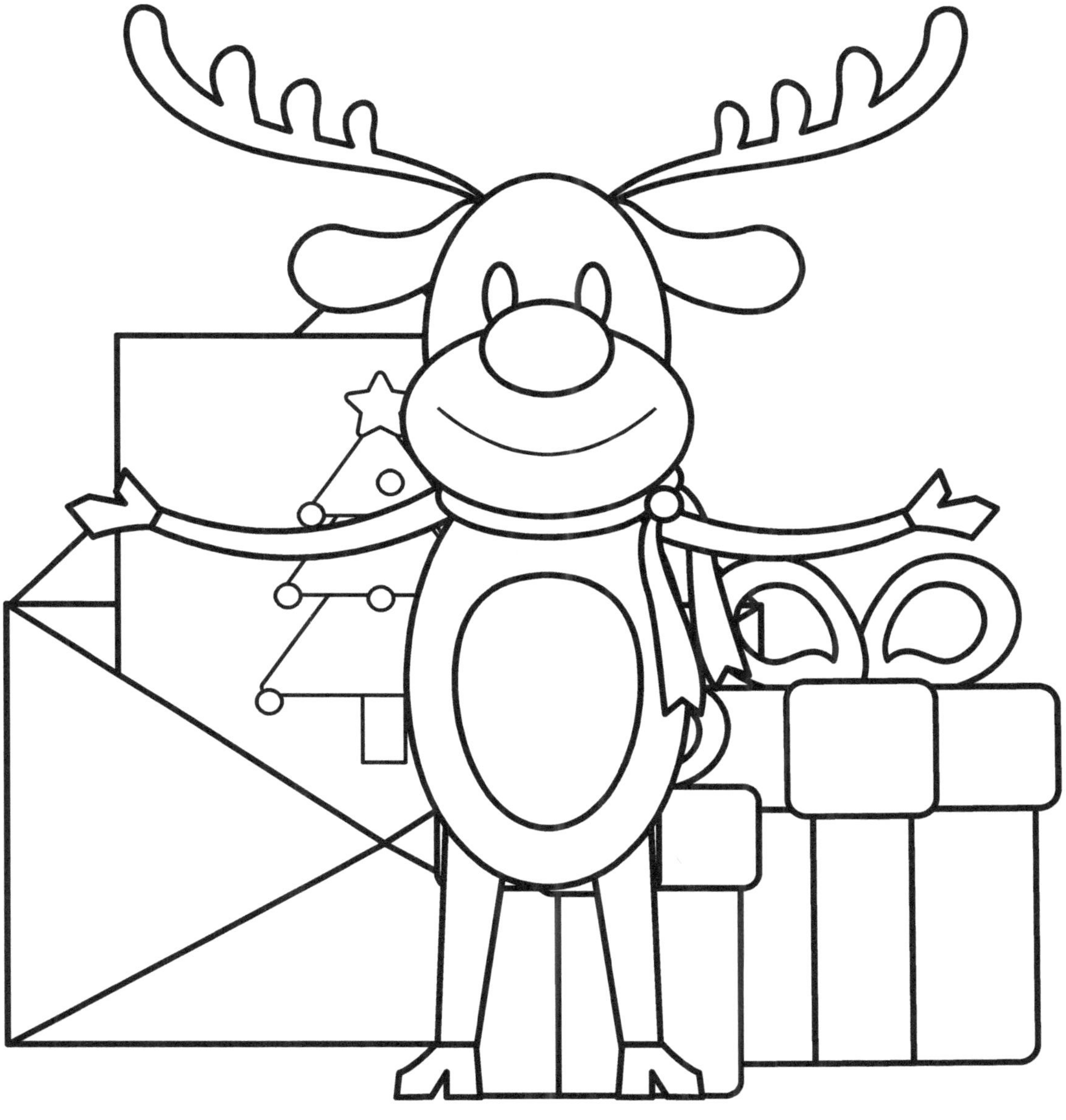

www.ingramcontent.com/pod-product-compliance
Lightning Source LLC
Chambersburg PA
CBHW080905220526
45466CB00011BA/3467
9798552730940